Terrific Trucks!

CONSTRUCTION TRUCKS

I0798983

Ursula Pang

PowerKiDS press.

PK Beginners

Let's work with construction trucks!

This is a bulldozer.

Bulldozers dig!

This is a dump truck.

Dump trucks move and dump stuff!

This is a concrete mixer.

Concrete is used to make buildings!

This is a crane truck.

徐工集团
ELF
ISUZU
FOTON

Crane trucks lift!

This is a drum roller.

Drum rollers make the road flat!

Published in 2026 by The Rosen Publishing Group, Inc.
2544 Clinton Street, Buffalo, NY 14224

Copyright © 2026 by The Rosen Publishing Group, Inc.

All rights reserved. No part of this book may be reproduced in any form without permission in writing from the publisher, except by a reviewer.

First Edition

Editor: Greg Roza
Book Design: Jeffrey Taylor

Photo Credits: Cover Johathan Weiss/Shutterstock.com; p. 3 AI generated image/Shutterstock.com; p. 5 Smileus/ Shutterstock.com; p. 7 Dmitry Kalinovsky/ Shutterstock.com; p. 9 AI generated image/Shutterstock.com; p. 11 AI generated image/Shutterstock.com; p. 13 Roman023_photography/Shutterstock.com; p. 15 AI generated image/Shutterstock.com; p. 17 Kondrelena/ Shutterstock.com; p. 19 Deek/Shutterstock.com; p. 21 Juan Wnrique del Barrio/Shutterstock.com; p. 23 Trong Nguyen/ Shutterstock.com.

Library of Congress Cataloging-in-Publication Data
Names: Pang, Ursula, author.
Title: Construction trucks / Ursula Pang.
Description: Buffalo : PowerKids Press, [2025] | Series: Terrific trucks!
Identifiers: LCCN 2024052610 (print) | LCCN 2024052611 (ebook) | ISBN 9781499451597 (library binding) | ISBN 9781499451580 (paperback) | ISBN 9781499451603 (ebook)
Subjects: LCSH: Trucks--Juvenile literature. | Construction equipment--Juvenile literature.
Classification: LCC TL230.15 .P359 2025 (print) | LCC TL230.15 (ebook) | DDC 629.225--dc23/eng/20241209
LC record available at https://lccn.loc.gov/2024052610
LC ebook record available at https://lccn.loc.gov/2024052611
Manufactured in the United States of America

Some of the images in this book illustrate individuals who are models. The depictions do not imply actual situations or events.

CPSIA Compliance Information: Batch #CSPK26. For further information contact Rosen Publishing at 1-800-237-9932.

Find us on